Silhouette

Nancy Viera

Silhouette

•

•

For James y para mi madre
You are my inspiration

-

-

-

Also by Nancy Viera

The Grief and The Happiness

Silhouette

Poems

Nancy Viera

I am

I am not what they want me to be
    I am not quite
    I am not timid
    I am not your construct
    I am not thin
    I am not fat
    I am not like you
    I am not a college degree
    I am not a job title
    I am not just a mother
    I am not just a woman
    I am who I am

Nancy Viera

The Cliff

I am at the precipice of the cliff
    Overwhelm takes over
    I take a few steps back
    Lift the weight of all the of the feelings
    The fears
    The overwhelm falls slowly as I take off my blue dress
    The one I never wore
    The sky clears above
    The color of the grass is brighter
    Fluffier
    Suddenly, big leaves sprout from my feet
    Enveloping me in safety
    My body is light and comforting
    The leaves protect me
    My path
    I take the leap
    The cliff takes me
    I am safe

Nancy Viera

.

.

Scent

When you died, a piece of me died
   It wasn't the part of me you met
   The charisma
   The laughter
   The love
   It wasn't the part of me that makes me resilient
   Strong
   Graceful
   Immense
   No, what died was beyond that
   It was the laughter that you brought me
   It was the scent only I recognize
   The inside jokes
   The unfinished conversations
   The one who picked up the phone
   It was the words only you and I knew
   The embrace that only lives in my memories now
   When you died so did everything I will never get back

Nancy Viera

Bounce

There is a lot of bounce to my step
My curls bounce on top of my head and down my back
Ideas brewing inside my head, bursting through every coil
There is a lot of bounce to my step
My callipygian beauty bouncing around showing the world the hips,
the curves
The movements I am made of, dancing down the street
There is a lot of bounce to my step
My chest bounces as I step reminding me
I am a sexy
ferocious creature
The beat of my heart dancing with every bounce
There is a lot of bounce to my step.
The way my belly seduces gravity when I strut
Not apologizing for its size
Bouncing with all its glory

Nancy Viera

.

Dad

I wonder, is he alive?
    Does he search my name on Google like I do his?
    Does he know I look just like him?
    I wonder if he knows the laugh
    The giggle of when I was a baby no longer exists?
    Does he wonder if I am stubborn like him
    A hard worker like him
    Persistent like him
    Does he know my eyes disappear when I smile?
    And when I cry
    I wonder does he look for me in crowds
    In his dreams
    I wonder
    Did he want to be my dad?

.

Nancy Viera

Curly

She thought, maybe if my curls are straight
   I will be more desirable
   They will accept me
   They will ask me to dance
   They won't notice the roundness of my stomach
   I will be like all the other ones, with their sleek hair
   Waterfalls upon their back
   Maybe I can fit in to their circles
   While I lose the kink of my coil
   while the shine leaves each strand
   Maybe they won't notice how loud my laugh is
   Or how I stare into the sky
    While they talk about mindless things
   Maybe they won't notice that as I lose my curl
    I lose my self
   I lose my wild
   I lose my purpose
   I lose my voice
   I lose my heart
   She thought
   Maybe if I keep my curls
   I won't have to lose anything

.

His Pain

I find beauty in the moments where I am to be lamenting instead

I find beauty in the pain as the wound once agape now closes

I find beauty in the line that dances with danger

I find beauty in the tear that rolls down your cheek

Releasing the terror from your cry

Your pain

I find beauty in the pain the heart feels as it breaks reminding me of life

I find beauty in the memory of wanting to leave everything behind and escape

I find beauty in the dream that swept me away and brought me back to life, to love

To be alive

.

Nancy Viera

Ghost

Sitting next to you outside the restaurant as the sun set on the day we met, felt like home

There was a familiarity in your eyes. Maybe we have met in a previous life

The way the first kiss lifted my feet off the earth and took me into the universe looping me into yours

A never ending hug sealed it for me

I haven't been able to breathe since the last time I saw you, I keep trying to catch my breath waiting for your next move

For the next time I will hear from you

Was I dreaming?

Did my brain have a lapse in time?

Were you a ghost?

Oh, I got your text. I hope that's the real excuse

I hope you feel better soon

.

Dirt

Crossing to unknown territory, you got into the crammed van trusting the strangers with your life. You swore you would do anything for me, and I didn't believe you. I was nineteen, you had just turned twenty years old. It wasn't until I called the neighbor with the only working phone in the small town we both grew up in that I knew you really would do anything for me. I could hear the askance as she told me you were held up in a detention center at the border. "He's probably being fed scraps and it's all your fault." She barked at me.

That summer, I begged my mother to let me come stay with my grandmother with her in San Borjas. It was my way of escaping the impending doom of nursing school. I hated blood, and it was her dream. Not mine.

Reminiscing on my childhood, and romanticizing the idea of living in Mexico was quickly interrupted when I noticed you.

There you were, across the street loading up the yellow old chevy. The sun beating down your back as you stacked up the hay bales. I plopped down on the hot cement fanning the hot air away with my baseball hat. I immediately noticed the curve of your dimples and the pout of your lips.

The syrup colored eyes enveloped me, and I wanted to

know more.

It was like falling asleep, slow, steady, then all at once the way we fell in love. Or whatever that was.

I'd pray for the days to fast forward, and for the nights to slow down. I was only allowed to see you in the evenings. We'd kiss for hours as soon as the sun went down always believing the sidewalk was our only witness.

My grandmother would scold me with lectures. "It's too much, too soon, what will people think?" I would disregard her lesson and look for you.

Romantic songs would bounce off the windows in the midnights of that summer. Promising eternal love, and to follow me wherever I went.

I was mostly grateful for the hot Sunday evenings because it meant I could ride in the yellow truck with you around the town plaza. You showed me off, you were proud to be seen with me. I was too. Sitting next to you, smiling, hands intertwined.

Then, reality woke us up like a cold bucket of ice. I had to return to the States and you couldn't follow me. Instead I watched you load your yellow chevy again, this time with my heavy bags.

We cried as I got on the cold metal bus that was taking me away. With the heavy smell of purple fabuloso you said you would follow me, sealing the promise with one last kiss.

I see you now, more than a decade later. I think you are happy. You are married now. You have three beautiful children and a wife, who now get to ride in your yellow truck.

Back

Tall linebacker, curls bursting through your Pittsburgh Steelers hat
   Sliding palms up and down looking for warmth with the friction
   The cold Sunday afternoon waits for the football game to start
   Gasping for air I sit behind you. The mile-high city in front of us
   Quick with the wit you smile back and tell me it's your first football game
   We smile with the sun blinding our eyes shut, sealing the rivalry with a picture together
   We banter at every interception
   Cheer when your offense gains yards
   In between goal kicks I admire your shoulders
   Your smile
   Your eyes
   With a charming smile you ask for my number when the game is over
   "I go back to Texas tomorrow, I have to go back to college"
   You must be fourteen years younger than me

What kind of Texas guy cheers for the Steelers?

Hat

Shiny neon vest, concrete smelling skin, rough hands, sweet smile. That is how I remember you. We met one hot summer evening at a rodeo. The dirt bounced off the floor as boots slid left to right. With one hand on your hip as you extended the other my way. "Bailamos?" you asked me to dance. To the beat of the cumbia you held me close to you, I drowned in the musk of your fresh pressed shirt, hints of fabric softener tickled my nose. "I am from Durango, we don't dance like that!" You said. "You Chihuahua girls think you can lead". Me being from Chihuahua had nothing to do with wanting to lead, I thought. You shifted my body in a steady motion. I looked up and found the dark of your eyes enchanting. The tan of your skin adoring.I know I broke your heart the way I so abruptly decided to end our relationship.

After a year, I could foresee a future where I wouldn't be living out my dreams, even if I wasn't quite sure what they were. I wanted to be a singer, a dancer, a teacher, a writer, a poet, a soldier, a cook. Housewife was not on the list. You said if I married you I would never have to work a day ever again. That I could stay home, cook, clean, tend to the five children we would have. I was scared of the idea. I just wanted to dance with you. You crossed my mind a few times. I saw you years later at a dance. One I attended alone. I meant to tell you, years later when you messaged me, asking if I was happy. I was. I am.

Through the bouncing couples I noticed you, tall, happy, handsome in the black stetson. A veil of dust through the light revealed your pregnant dancing partner. I smiled, you got what you wanted.

Sin

Sitting on the hot school bus I was sleepy and annoyed. As I tossed my curls into a bun I could feel you staring. "With those eyes, and my eyes, we'd make cute babies." You flirted.

I rolled my eyes and ignored you. The dust of the bus separated us.

Fourteen years later there you are again. Heartbroken and newly divorced. I tell myself it will be just a hookup so we meet up at a hotel.

The smell of your cologne danced around my body enabling senses I had forgotten existed. Your hands knew exactly where to go, my body responded without hesitation.

Your marble eyes stared into my soul, as you gripped my hair, I gasped for air. Our lips connected like two missing puzzle pieces. Shit. This isn't just a hookup.

Two months later we board a plane that takes us on a trek to the land of sins and hot breath.

Vegas is our witness. We walked the streets, sometimes your hand on my bottom, sometimes intertwined with mine. We laugh as the street performers steal me away from you for a quick snap. Drink like fools and get lost in our bodies back at the hotel room. Our reverie.

I can't help but cry. Sitting at the top of the stratosphere overlooking the city lights, your arm around me feels surreal.

"Yeah, I didn't think I'd be here sitting next to you like this, either."

You console me.

We sin, we love, we move on.

Flow

I used to go down to the river to dip my toes
   To wash my clothes
   To look for rocks
   I'd cradle the rock
   It was my baby
   I'd meet my friends
   We would dip our toes
   Wash our clothes
   Look for rocks
   I used to go down to the river
   To dip my toes
   Wash my clothes
   Look for rocks
   Meet my love
   He kissed my toes
   Took off my clothes
   And then it all flowed
   I used to go down to the river when I was a girl
   And then, I became a woman
   I never went back to the river

.

Cross

I hate when I leave her behind
   With the baby on her arms
   With uncertainty ahead of me
   With the vast river to cross
   I hate leaving behind me
   The love
   The comfort
   Even the red sauce
   I hate not knowing my return
   So I kiss them one more time
   I hate when I leave everything behind
   Even myself
   I hope when I see them again
   I can change the paradigm
   I hope
   I never leave again

Exhale

The ocean takes a breath
　　and then it holds it
　　As the wave holds its tremble
　　I walk the path in between my dreams and my fears
　　I caress the twinkle of the water
　　A drop on my finger begs me to please let her exhale
　　What she doesn't know is that while she stands still
　　I see my life twirl all around me
　　The love
　　The betrayal
　　The healing
　　I see my reflection on her tender foam
　　It reveals my hearts desire
　　I take a step back
　　Then
　　The ocean exhales

.

Tall

You were in my dreams again last night
    So stoic
    So handsome
    So gentle
    So strong
    Your eyes seemed gentle when I tried to touch your face
    It faded on to the next scene
    You were laughing
    You made me laugh
    I reached again to touch your face
    This time you grabbed my hand
    I felt your love crawl through every cell
    Then, you faded again
    This time I woke up
    You were in my dreams again last night
    But, why aren't you here instead?

Nancy Viera

Jealous

I sit under the tree
    Its shadow blankets a cool breeze over my shoulders
    The sun is boiling above me
    He is sad
    He is heartbroken
    In my shelter, I look up at his blinding light
    And his sorrow comes down in every ray
    I thank him for spilling sunshine down my face
    On the flowers
    On the shimmer of the creek
    He remains melancholic
    The day begins to tuck him away
    He paints the sky with shadows
    The people awaken
    They dance under the moonlight
    and the summer breeze she brings
    The sun from the other side grows jealous with heat

.

Stay

He always comes back to me during the summer
   When my body is bare
   When my skin is softer
   When my hair is wilder
   He comes back seeking the cool shelter
    that my love offers
   The tenderness of my body
   Melts him more than the boiling sun
   His skin sinks into mine
   Pours his soul inside me
   Warm and loving
   An exquisite retreat
   He runs his fingers
   through the coils and vines
   atop my head
   As his fingers get stuck reality wakes him
   He can't stay
   He doesn't know how to stay
   I watch him fade in to the bright sunshine,
   I know he will be back
   He always comes back to me during the summer

.

Curve

Let me tell you about the curve of your lips
    The thump of your step
    The thunder of your heart
    Let me tell you about the leap of my soul
    The crashing of my light
    The crawl when you touch me
    A twinkle takes over
    It brings the elixir to my lips
    All the way down to my toes
    Oh how I longed the release
    Of my breath next to yours
    Can this be it
    The moment I've dreamed
    The moment I've craved
    Are you really here
    I want to tell you everything now that you are here
    I want to get lost in the curve of your being

Voice

Look over there, she said
   Through the eye of the hill
   The bark of the tree
   Do you see it?
   Look over there, where the river meets the concrete
   Where the rocks pile up
   Do you see the twinkle of the sun kissing the puddle
   Look again
   Beyond the meadows
   Beyond the corn fields
   Do you hear the echo yet?
   Is that where you left it?
   Walkthrough the hot concrete
   Cross the river
   Disturb the twinkle
   Reach the top of the hill
   Take off the load
   Let the clothes scatter on the dirt
   Scream
   Sing
   Cry
   Do you hear that?

Your voice?
Its right where you left her

.

Copy

There is not one ounce of me that wishes to be
   Anything like you
   And a million reasons
   I want to be just like my self

.

.

Resistance

I stopped resisting when it started to feel good
    When the heavy cinder lifted
    My shoulders relaxed
    My heart sighed
    I stopped resisting when I was able to breath again
    When it got easier
    When the words flowed
    When the air was thinner
    I stopped resisting when the healing was the answer

.

Nancy Viera

Adobe

Her house was made out of adobe
  The mud was always warm
  I would sit on the wood chair she painted white
  The Virgen Maria stared at me from the wall
  My bisabuela clapping the potato mash
  Between her wrinkled tender hands
  I sat there with bright eyes
  Savoring the scent or the grease
  Savoring the tender grace of her eyes
  Gliding from one end of the kitchen to the other
   In tattered slippers
  Her favorite
  Now, she looks at me different
  She doesn't remember me
  She doesn't remember any of us
  She is lost in the memories of adobe and hot grease

Nancy Viera

.

.

Manic

She is fragile
    She is manipulative
    She is always sick
    But nothing is wrong with her
    She has those sweet eyes
    They cross like daggers
    She tells me she loves me
    But I know she is disappointed
    I am not her
    I am not her dreams
    I am not who she wants me to be
    I am not her daughter

.

Nancy Viera

.

Barrier

I see her looking around
   Pacing around
   She looks nervous
   Picks up the lipstick
   Puts it back down
   Sweat starts to run down
   The sales man approaches
   Flawless skin
   Pale
   The eyes judge
   The arms cross
   Forming the barrier
   I lock eyes with her, and she sweats even more
   Yo hablo español, le ayudo?
   The breath of relief leaves her body
   She is looking for a darker shade of lipstick
   That is all

.

.

Canvas

Deep blue mountains
   The canvas to your silhouette
   Your lips
   Your smile stands out
   Your glance envelops me
   Shoulder leaning
   Music blasting
   Conversation flowing
   Can I freeze this frame
   Can I freeze this feeling
   How can someone look so beautiful when driving

.

Nancy Viera

.

Parted

I managed to convince my lips to part
   Take you in
   Close my eyes
   Meet my nightmares in the twilight
   No one forced me to be here
   No one said I had to do it
   I managed to convince myself
   This was the only way
   To be loved
   To be touched
   To feel
   I managed to convince myself
   The only way was with you there

Nancy Viera

Found

There is something in the way she kept looking for it
    Wading through the crowds
    Screaming at the top
    Every time she changed her hair
    When she took that road trip
    In the songs playing on the stereo
    Every time she changed jobs
    She searched for it in the books
    The movies
    The cold
    The wet
    There was something in the way
    she kept looking for it
    When they kissed her
    Took her clothes off
    When they left her
    There was something powerful
    when she finally looked in the mirror
    And knew that what she was looking
    for was not in the crowd
    The top of the mountain

Or her hair
The songs were beautiful
The road breathtaking
It was not it
Her truth all along was in her heart
Her voice
Her silhouette

.

Sticky

Shiny sticky lipstick
   Blue long hair
   Curled and burned
   Arrogance envelops the big necklace that sits on her small chest
   Shielding the heart of stone
   She has lost her tenderness
   The humble
   The soft
   They made her this way
   When they laughed
   When they pushed
   When they ignored
   Now, her shield is her clothes
   Her books
   Her knowledge
   Now she belittles anyone who is beneath her
   Is she better now
   Or just as worse

Nancy Viera

.

Change

I wish I could tell the summer to keep the scent
    The smoke of the camp
    Put it in a bottle
    Toss it in a lake
    I'd pick it up later
    When everyone is away
    I wish I could tell her to keep her smile
    Her wit
    Put it in a bottle
    Toss it down the mountain
    I'd pick it up when uncertainty dances
    When nothing makes sense
    I'd tell her to change the small ways she leaves her self
    Open up the bottle
    Come back to her self

.

Whiskey

Drenched in sweat
   With the heavy burden
   He puts down the horse mount
   His eyes are tired
   Yet he smiles
   Melancholy his shield
   He rubs my head
   The best type of love
   The rough hands
   Tender yet strong
   He quites the day with the sweet elixir
   Dear sir
   Please don't leave
   I don't want to grieve

Mirror

No one abandoned her
   When they ignored her
   When they left
   And came back on their terms
   No one abandoned her when she bore the responsibility
   Of being a mother as a child
   No one abandoned her when he strikes across her face
   When they picked someone prettier
   Someone smaller
   No one was there
   When she picked her self up
   When she decided to be present
   No one can abandon you
   When you've abandoned yourself

.

Nancy Viera

.

Do

I do it right
  I do it wrong
  I do it with my eyes closed
  I take the leap
  Never look back
  I do whatever I want

.

Nancy Viera

Knees

Who am I when you are not looking?
    Am I boring?
    Am I condescending?
    Am I extravagant?
    Am I aloof?
    How would you know?
    Outside these walls
    The walls you keep me in
    How would you know
    How gregarious I am
    How irresistible I am
    How unforgettable I am
    How would you know
    If you never look
    Past my head on your lap
    My eyes closed
    How would you know
    You only want me
    When I am on my knees

Nancy Viera

.

Brave

There are rows of magic ahead
   Masked in the cornfield
   The sun beats her every cell
   She picks up the bucket
   Full of hopes and rocks
   Her hat full of dreams
   None belong in this land
   She doesn't dream of meadows
   She dreams of concrete petals
   Rows of magic
   Instead, her future is tragic
   She should have stayed
   Where she was
   With the rows of magic

.

Nancy Viera

Soul

Your naked truth sits in front of me
   The oasis I've been seeking for
   Through the sleepless nights
   The trenches of my hopes
   There you are the million and infinite
   The desire
   The quench
   The alignment
   Let me sit in the puddle of your truth
   Of your voice
   Of your grace
   The truth of you rains directly into my soul

.

Nancy Viera

.

Purpose

I left my heart on a plane
   I couldn't see his face, damn that mask
   Damn this pandemic
   His brown eyes told me all the stories I needed to know
   The murmur was loud
   The tension louder
   We were on the same plane
   Just different destinations
   Our hearts, however, had found their home
   I left my heart on a plane
   With the memory of the conversation
   With the memory of the connection
   He lives his purpose
   I float looking for redirection
   To return to the place where I left my heart
   Next to his imperfection

.

.

Seasons

It was Summer
    She was wild
    She was fire
    Her love, quick to spread like wildfires
    Her thirst only quenched by summer flings
    Then
    It was Fall
    The tender leaves wrapper her toes
    Asking for forgiveness
    They didn't mean to change
    To freeze on the ground
    To die
    Then
    It was Winter
    The frost pinched her nose
    The twinkle of the lights brought her love again
    Then
    When all the flowers and leaves returned
    She hid
    She feared that with the fires
    With the fall

And the frost
They would leave her again

.

Until next time

Xoxo

Silhouette

.

.

.

Nancy Viera

.

Thank you

I'd like to express my deepest gratitude to the land that saw me grow up. San Francisco de Borja is a small enchanting town in Chihuahua Mexico. It sits nestled in between hills and the river Conchos. If you ever get the opportunity to visit, go during October and visit the beautiful Canyon de Namurachi. Make sure you visit the church, I've always thought it was full of secrets. Maybe we can delve more into that in the magical realism novel I have in the works.

Make friends, the people are warm and welcoming, I hope someone invites you in for pan con cafe.

The town is home to natives of the Raramuri Tribes, and the land where my ancestors rest. A lot of my poems are written while thinking of this town. Mi Pueblo, always in my heart.

Thank you to the Quilt community. For holding space, for the support and the love. You inspire me. Quilt is an audio social media community that I highly encourage you to find. Search your App Store for Quilt.

Thank you Sara Candela for being inspiration and magic all in one human.

The Open Mic crew for motivating me to write, and for the best cheers I've ever received.

Thank you to all the men I've written about in my poems, for the lessons, the rejections, and for giving me a story to tell. You always come back. Please stop. Except you, you know who you are.

Thank you to my readers. I am honored to have a place in your bookshelf.

.

Silhouette

Also by Nancy Viera, The Grief and The
Happiness

DEATH

I can't get up. If I get up, I will die. If I die, my son will be motherless, and that can't happen because he is also fatherless. The air is thick as the sun peeks rays right on my eyes. The heavy blanket of responsibility sits on my body as I open my eyes on a breezy summer morning. At 34, I didn't imagine I'd be raising a son on my own. I lift my heavy head and slide across the room to the bathroom where I splash my face with cold water. I start the shower, look in the mirror, and white hair pops out from one of my brown curls. Frizz all over. With a heavy sigh, I wash away the nightmares that haunt me from the night. I walk into my son's room and lightly slide the curtains open letting the rays come through the window, hitting his sweet, warm face. "It's a good morning, time to wake up!" I squeeze his face and wish he was a baby again. I wish my son's innocence had not been robbed. He opens his big brown eyes and smiles, puts a finger up to protest for wanting to stay in bed longer, his face marked from the blankets of his slumber.

After a long day of work and summer school, we make our way to Fort Logan National Cemetery to visit his dad. Half his ashes are buried among other soldiers, the other half float in the Gulf of Mexico. He caresses the cold marble with his fingers running through the crevices of his dad's engraved name. His eyes drop down deep into the wet earth. James is ten years old. We are visiting his father, his namesake, on the eve of another Father's Day without him. It's been four years since Jim died.

He looks up at me, with watery eyes and a soft smile. A soft breeze hugs the air. He asks me the question I have been dreading since the day I discovered Jim's cause of death.

During the Spring of 2016, I decided to take a week off from work and take my son on a fun trip. I had saved the money to splurge on one day at Disneyland. It was all I could afford at the time. My inner child was squealing with happiness. I was so happy to be taking my son on our first trip together. His dad and I were divorced. He lived in Florida after finally returning stateside from a four year on and off deployment to a war zone.

On the day of our trip, I sent Jim several text messages asking him to call us back. No answer. I followed by sending a video of James dancing in the living room clapping his hands and shaking his body to a bluegrass beat. He was so excited. Still no answer. I sent him a message on social media "Are you okay?"

Now I was worried. My gut told me something wasn't right. On the drive to the airport, I wondered if he had a woman over and didn't want me to know. I didn't care, I just wanted him to talk to his son.

After persisting a few times more with no response, I finally received a voicemail.

"This is Zach, Jim's roommate, I have something to tell you," he said with a solemn tone.

We were in line at airport security now, my heart began to beat faster. As soon as I got my shoes back on, wiped the sweat off my forehead I called Jim's phone back. Zach answered again.

"What's going on? Is he playing a prank on me to ruin our trip?" I said to him with a nervous laugh in my voice. My body tensed up preparing for the worst.

"No, I can tell you it's not a prank. Where are you? Are you with family?" he patiently asked.

"No, we are on our way to California. What's going on?" I asked, now flustered as we walked through the busy terminal.

I heard a heavy sigh. "Jim passed away. We found him yesterday unresponsive."

I stopped walking, looked down at James who was holding my hand. I wanted to collapse to my knees right in between gates A39 to A49. The sweet hand holding mine reminded me I had to be strong. My mouth felt dry. I felt heavy, the way you drag heavy furniture across a room. My mind went blank and everything around me stopped moving.

Zach's voice woke me up. He asked if I was okay. I let him know I couldn't discuss details and hung up the phone. This moment is when I became the strongest person I have ever known myself to be. Not for me, for my son.

We walked over to our gate. I handed James a book to read as we waited to board the plane. I looked at my phone. The first person I wanted to call was Jim. I called my Mom instead. She was in Mexico at the time building her house, a dream of hers.

I needed to tell someone Jim was dead, and no one was

going to console me when I was not allowing myself to break down. "Tu eres fuerte. Tú sabrás cuándo decirle a James las palabras saldrán de tu corazón. Sigan con su viaje, su cuerpo está lejos y tú ya hiciste lo que pudiste lo más difícil te espera."

"Go on your trip. Be strong for your son. You will know the right time to tell him. Right now, his body is in Florida. You can figure everything else when you get back. The hardest is yet to come," she consoled me.

I felt my chest tighten. All I could think of was Jim lifeless. It seemed like a heavy dream. As I buckled my seatbelt and fastened James', I felt all my insides go to war with themselves. I kept picturing Jim's body cold, stiff, in a lonely morgue room. I wondered who the last person was to touch him when he was alive. Who was the last to kiss him or hug him?

I couldn't make sense of why he was dead. Was it happening? Was he really dead?

I tilted my head back on the small plane seat, closed my eyes hoping to wake up from the dreadful abyss I seemed to be falling into.

During the flight, I kept looking at my little guy fighting the lump in my throat. I knew the moment was not right. I needed the right words to tell him, to break his heart. Once we landed my phone kept ringing, but the only person I wanted to talk to was now dead. I kept telling myself to not break down.

The next day we went to Disneyland and the first picture I took of James was near the magical princess castle. As I snapped the picture, he immediately asked me to send it to his dad. "I will. Let's take a lot of pictures, that way we can save the battery for sending later," I replied.

After every ride, he would gleefully tell me to call his dad. He wanted to tell him how much fun he was having. "I don't think he is available to talk right now, Papa (my nickname for little James). His phone might not be working. Here, let's go on this ride." I led him to Tomorrowland, ironically. I couldn't lie to him. I did not want to. I kept getting calls and text messages, and I kept ignoring them. I could not talk to anyone about it at that moment, I was leading my son through the happiest place on earth. I was not about to break down crying and ruin his day, just yet.

I yearned for the moment of ignorance. The moments in between phone calls when I didn't know what was happening. When I didn't know that Jim was dead. I so badly wanted it to be a bad dream that I could wake up from. I wanted to be stuck in the in-between. I kept shoving down any feeling crawling up my throat.

When we got back to the hotel, after the festive fireworks show, I waited until James fell asleep before I locked myself in the echo of the hotel bathroom. I ran a hot shower and finally broke down while the water scorched my skin. I regretted not hugging Jim longer several months before when he visited us for a few days. I regretted not being there more for him. I began to blame myself. If I would have never divorced him, our life, his life wouldn't have ended like this. Now my son would not have a father, someone to teach him all the cool "bro stuff" I couldn't teach him. Was this my fault? But I had nothing to do with his death.

As I braided my wet hair, James slept in the bed next to me, tired from a day of magical moments and uncounted smiles. My son was six years old when I broke his heart. I was the one responsible for delivering the heartbreak and needed all the strength I could manage to do so. What would I say to comfort him? At the time I did not know the cause, so what would I say was the reason? I couldn't lie to him. These questions brewed in my head all night and throughout the morning. I looked for solace by posting that question on social media while at the same time telling the world Jim was dead before I told his son.

We went to Huntington Beach the next morning, he ran straight to the water without fear and frolicked for a few hours. Dread filled my heart as he walked up to me, his hair dripping cold water, because I knew what he would ask me next.

"Can we please call daddy now?" he insisted. I knew right there was the time to tell him. The beach was deserted for the most part, with a few people walking in the distance, enjoying their peaceful stroll while I worked up the courage to talk to James. I sat him in front of me, grasping his face. I looked him straight in his eyes and told him his dad was dead. I broke my son's heart to the sound of crashing waves and seagulls screaming. I comforted him as he laid in my arms, digging my feet in the hot sand. He did not cry much; he was just solemn. It was heartbreaking.

"So, his heart just stopped working?" was his first question.

I nodded and grabbed his sweet face again. "You have me, I will help you get through this. You have Wita, Grandpa, Sarai, Valery, Amelia, and a lot of people that love you and will be there for you."

I knew at that moment he lost a lot of his innocence and took it upon himself to be strong. He became the strongest person I've ever met. His resilience amazed me that day, and to this day I am more in awe of him.

"Mom, how did dad really die?" James asks me that question as we sit on at the foot of his dad's grave.

That question haunts my thoughts almost every day. I was tasked with keeping his Dad's memory alive. Jim would often ask me to make sure James remembered him every day, and so I do.

He just turned ten, but every time I talk to him it feels like he is older. I often find myself amazed at his maturity and high level of understanding. But that question, I am not ready to talk about with him yet. So, instead, I hug him and ask him for time.

I met Jim in late 2008, by the end of it we were married and crazy in love. He was stationed in Fort Carson, Colorado, and I was sleeping on my friend's couch. Earlier that year, my friends and I were planning to have a house party until someone suggested we go out to dance instead. My gut feeling was to say no right away, and this was unheard of by me. I loved going out to dance, I've been going out dancing since I was fifteen; so many cute guys to look at! It only took a few looks from my friends and I fulfilled their capricious wishes. We smeared the make-up extra heavy, put on the cutest shirt we could choose, and walked into the night club dancing.

When we arrived at the club, I rejected the drinks offered to me and went straight to the dance floor. Shaking my hips and head to the beat I was happy to be there dancing with my friends without a worry. I got a phone call and stepped off the dance floor to answer. I was expecting to meet up with more friends and they needed directions.

A fight broke out several feet away from me. I looked over, and that's when I felt a sting in my eye. My vision went dark. Someone threw a beer bottle and it hit the right side of my face. My friends rushed me to the bathroom. I assured them it was only a sting, I felt okay.

Monica took a small pocket mirror and handed it to me. "Look at your face, Nancy. It's worse than it feels. We are taking you to the hospital!" Panic set in all of their eyes.

As my friends rushed me out of the building, I saw two guys being escorted out of the club. No marks on their faces. They didn't get arrested, just thrown out.

Monica rushed me to the emergency room. Handing me a cigarette she kept looking at my face. "It's going to be okay, babe," she said switching the clutch of her little red car. The worried look on her face told me otherwise. I kept my hand on my eye and hoped for the best.

The beer bottle hit and broke my orbital eye floor, scarring my retina. To this day, I have a huge cloud on my right eye that prevents me from being able to see out of it. For this reason, my mom kicked me out of the house, or so I told myself. I was twenty-something and thought I knew better. When she came to visit me in the hospital as I awaited surgery, she told me how disappointed she was. I cried, laying on the hospital bed with rough sheets. I longed for her hug and her approval.

"This is what I raised you to do? This is how you end up?" her voice full of scorn and shame.

"I wasn't even drinking, Mama. I was just at the wrong place the wrong time. It was an accident."

This didn't convince her. In her eyes, I was a disgrace. After she left, I had a drug-induced dream. In the dream, she threatened to take me home and lay me out on the couch so all my family could see what I ended up like. I didn't have a husband and children. I was nothing to her and our family. The next morning, she came back to check on me. In fear of my dream coming true, I told her I was going to live with my friend Kiki and asked her to leave the hospital room.

"The next time I see you, you will be in a casket." My mom looked down and walked out.

The next day after recovering from surgery, Kiki and Monica were waiting for me. They lent me clothes and gave me a place to sleep on their couch. I'd take turns with Kiki's mom watching television and cooking food before going back to work. For months, Kiki would drive me to work until I was able to ride the bus. I had lost my car in previous months because I thought it was okay to skip paying the bill for a few months. I was young and stupid.

Because of my accident, my work performance quality decreased significantly. E-mails went unanswered and my boss noticed. I was put on a probationary period. The scare from the accident and being put on probation for the job I loved reignited my work ethic and by the end of the year, I was a top performer.

While I was excelling at work, the confidence that once radiated from my eyes left me, and I began looking for validation in the wrong places. This is when I met Jim. Half of my face was disfigured with a broken orbital floor, a scarred retina, half-blind, all of my confidence was gone. Yet he still loved being around me. He didn't care what my face looked like. He liked my personality and I fell in love with his gregarious wit, red hair, his beautiful big chocolate eyes, and the way he towered over me. He wore his strength like armor. I loved being in his arms. His hugs put me back together when I felt broken.

I met him on a dating website, a very inappropriate one at that. The truth is, I wasn't looking for a one-night stand, I've always been looking for love. Jim charmed me by saying I looked just like his type; Latina with big eyes and a big butt. He fired some Spanish words at me, and that's all it took for me to want to meet him in person.

Kiki drove me down in her blue mini cooper to Fort Carson to meet him in person. We drove around for a while lost until he spotted us, and jumped out of his car to stop ours. Standing tall, with his striped shirt and blue jeans, he opened his arms. I fell in love right in the middle of Harr Avenue, cars honking at us while we kissed.

When I was younger, I pictured my future with one person. My grey hair would appear, and I would be running around with my husband spoiling our grandchildren. In my vision, we would sit on the porch and read books while sipping on tea, or whiskey. When I met Jim, I felt like we were meant to be together for a short time. I knew I was in for a crazy ride, but I stayed. Because Jim was on active duty at the time he lived in the barracks. I'd often visit him there, and my friend Kiki came along. One day we sat in the living room area waiting for Jim, while he took a shower after a long shift, and for his friend to arrive since we had plans to go on a double date.

I noticed Jim's phone kept ringing. I picked it up to see if it was an emergency and because I was curious. It was no emergency, only about twenty text messages coming through as I opened the grey flip phone. I read one of the conversations. I noticed it was a lot like the conversations I was would have with him. He called them "baby" just like he called me baby. I closed the phone and put it back on the shelf where it sat before. I lowered my eyes with disappointment.

"Let's go home, you deserve a guy who is not texting ten other girls, Nancy," my friend Kiki said to me.

"No, I belong here, for now," I brushed her off. I knew I had to stay with him, for now. My gut feeling told me I belonged there.

After dating for two months, we decided to get married one weekend after I introduced Jim to my family at Thanksgiving dinner. Jim was house-sitting for one of his Army buddies and I helped with the dog. While we were walking the dog that weekend, Jim looked at me and asked me if I wanted to get married, nothing romantic.

The following Monday at the El Paso County Courthouse, we held hands as a judge pronounced us husband and wife. Once outside the courthouse, we both cried. It felt so surreal to be husband and wife. As a celebration, we went to grab grilled sandwiches, and then I dropped him off back at work.

I drove back to Denver and on the way there the first person I called was my grandma in Mexico. She was so happy for us. And of course, the first question she asked is when we planned to have children and when we would visit her in Mexico. But she knew me. My life never followed a typical path. Whatever that means.

Jim and I would spend most weekends together. I lived in Denver, so we had a long-distance marriage for two months. I loved the drives around Colorado Springs scaring people with a loud air horn. James was driving, drinking my big gas station cup filled with iced tea. He loved iced tea.

"Why are we stopping at the hardware store?" I asked him with a puzzled look on my face.

"Just wait, it's going to be hilarious." I sat in the truck waiting for him to come back, excited to know what he was up to.

He got back into the truck with the most mischievous smile on his face. "I need you to drive and slow down every time I tell you to." He ordered, so I obliged.

HOOOOOOOOONK! he fired the air horn at me, and I cackled with him. It was on. We drove around downtown Colorado Springs for hours just honking the air horn at random strangers and laughing hysterically at their reactions.

We spent a lot of days laughing and a lot of days arguing. I'll never forget the numerous pranks he played on me and the ones I fired back at him.

"You know we are going to have the cutest kids, right?" he would tell me. "But before we have those kids, I will take you to Spain and we will dance the nights away." He took me out dancing years later. We never made it to Spain. Three months after we got married, we found out little James was on the way.

"Oh, it's going to be a boy," we both said right away. Fear and happiness trembled in our voices.

When you are in the military and married, they supply on-base housing or stipends. We lived in an apartment off-base, but Jim quickly got us a house at the Fort Carson Army Base so we could be close to the hospital and his work. That summer he moved our couches, bed, tables, and boxes all on his own. He had a crazy strength to him. We set up, and settled into, our new home.

Some days he would cook his famous pulled pork sandwiches and sometimes I sent him off to work with Carne con Papas (meat with potatoes). He'd often comment how lucky he was that he married into a Latin family, and the great culinary skills I had. We spent a lot of time going out for walks and he would always fail at convincing me to do the steep hikes around Colorado Springs.

"Boy, what's wrong with you, this belly is bigger than my head, I am not hiking up anything right now." Jim would make fun of my accent, and I'd make fun of the way he said, "alrighty" instead of okay. I loved spending time with Jim.

At night, he would disappear into his headset and game controller, arguing with angsty teenagers via online video games.

I was heavy into my third trimester during the summer. I laid on the couch with the fan humming air at me, when my neighbor walked in and cackled.

"Oh, girl! I remember those pregnant days. You must be so hot!"

She hauled me off to the pool on the base where I floated gleefully and cooled off. Her husband was deployed to a war zone and she shared stories of struggle and laughter. We became instant friends. She shared her Puerto Rican dishes while I showed off my Mexican cuisine skills. We were military wives. Over a decade later, we are still good friends.

During my last month of pregnancy, I was put on bed rest. Jim would bring me food during his lunchtime and check on me as many times as possible. He would call me two to three times a day, even if we were fighting. On the day I was induced, I got to pin James for his promotion and then head to the hospital right after. Fourteen hours later, a big-eyed cherub with red hair, and big brown eyes was born, and everything seemed right with the world.

For the first nine months of our son's life, we were learning a lot about raising a little man. At the same time, we were trying to figure out what Jim's next career move would be as his contract with the Army was up. He ultimately decided to sign up for another term with a different unit and before our son's first birthday, we loaded him on a bus to Iowa to a unit that was deploying to Afghanistan. Our family was never the same and would never reunite to the bliss we had before deployment. One very cold November morning after little James was born, Jim woke me up from my slumber at four in the morning, the smell of crunchy tortillas filled the air.

"I made breakfast burritos and we are going on a drive. Get the baby boy ready," he said, very content with himself.

I didn't question him. Drives with him were always an adventure. We drove through Cheyenne Mountain State Park and ended up in a very beautiful rocky area where we could watch the sunrise. Again, he suggested we hike, and again, I refused.

We happily ate our burritos while the sun rose over Colorado Springs with little James still deep in sleep. I remember we sat in silence for awhile. Jim had a way of saying a lot in his silence. He stared at me for a few minutes. It made me wish I could read his mind.

He looked down and said, "I am just not sure how long we will make it Nancy. I do not feel like I have everything you and Chancho deserve and I want to give you the life you deserve." Jim liked to call little James "Chancho".

I let Jim talk as I listened with my heart breaking a little, feeling him slip away. I wanted to tell him that we deserved to give it a try and not give up because of uncertainty or fears. That no matter what, our little family would make it through anything. But I could see the defeat in his eyes. It wasn't the time for us to end our marriage. He was about to deploy, and I was going to be left to take care of a child on my own. With my family in Denver, and his in Florida, I had very little support and his words ached throughout my heart. I looked down and kept quiet.

One day after I came back from work, he sat me down in the dining room and told me he found a unit in Iowa with the caveat that they would be deploying soon. I cried, but I also knew that deployment was always a possibility, so I supported him in his decision.

Within a week we moved out of the Army post housing into an apartment right off Fort Carson base. We used almost all of our money to put down a deposit, moving costs, and other fees that the Army would reimburse us for, but if you know anything about the Army, you're going to sit and wait a lot.

The day he had to leave, our friend Anna offered to do a photoshoot of our little family at Foxrun Park. She was able to capture a moment between my two guys. Jim was holding James in his arms, nuzzling on little James' neck and a bit of anguish can be seen in both their faces as if foreshadowing a sad future. This was the defining moment where the separation from father to soldier began.

With sixty dollars in his pocket, we dropped him off at the greyhound station in downtown Colorado Springs. We held onto each other with so much pain in our hearts as he was deploying to go to war. He stepped on the bus, and just like in the movies he stopped and looked back at us, standing near the entrance to the building. He mouthed, "I love you" and disappeared into the cold bus.

Jim arrived in Iowa for a family night dinner for the unit. He knew no one in that place until he met Joseph. Blue-eyed Joseph was making sure none of his sisters were getting hit on by the other soldiers. Joseph's mom saw Jim was alone and invited him to sit at their table. Shortly after, Joseph walked up to the table and asked, "who the fuck is this guy?"

Jim fired back by making jokes at Joseph's expense. They immediately became friends or "instant homie status", as Joseph told me years later, after Jim died.

A few years after Jim's death, we were invited to a unit reunion by his commanding officer. We got to meet several of the men and women who served with Jim in Afghanistan. As I was sipping on my drink, Rick approached me and asked how we were doing after Jim's death. I always hesitate right before answering this question. Do I say the truth of what's on my mind? Am I doing okay?

"We are doing okay. I still can't grasp why Jim kept deploying to a war zone. I guess he really liked it over there," I said sarcastically, but Rick corrected me. He explained that Jim probably didn't like the war zone. But that after you've been there once, it's hard to come back to civilian life. He spoke highly of Jim and said he had pretty much made himself indispensable. Jim was so good at his job that other agencies sought after him. I swirled around the ice cubes in my cup and took in his words. I looked around at the rest of the soldiers at the reunion. They all had different stories to tell. I kept picturing Jim around them and wished he was here with his comrades now.

* * *

I can't compare anything to being a soldier deployed to a war zone. I've only been on this side of the computer screen always waiting, always praying. The worst and most intense feelings came when Jim and I would be on video calls, the loud thunder of bombs would go off and he would get disconnected from the call. With the screen black in front of me, I'd stare almost afraid to imagine what happened.

When a bomb goes off near a camp in a war zone, the internet will be off for some days due to a blackout. There were times I wouldn't hear from him for two weeks or more. At least during the time when Jim was in a war zone that was the way it was. To show us he was alive, Jim would post a joke on Facebook or send me some silly video for me to laugh at, and then all would be right with the world…until the next attack. These are just some of the things you grow accustomed to when your husband is in a war zone. And yet, you are still surprised every time the thunderous bombs go off during a phone call.

We were lucky to have technology on our side when Jim was deployed. We would video chat often, but he also did the sweetest thing. Jim would write me letters. I save those letters for our son to read one day. Even if he finds them gross, I want him to see there was a time when his mom and dad loved each other so much that they wrote letters to each other.

Nancy,

       This is the letter I always promised you.

I wanted to tell you thank you for your love and gratitude. In just a few years we have grown as a couple and individuals.

I could search the world for the rest of my life and never find a woman that comes close to how perfect you are.

For me, it doesn't matter anyway because I am done looking. I am your loving and loyal husband forever.

Love,

  James

Nancy,

I walked all over looking for a pay phone and couldn't find one on campus. I walked for two hours. I was so depressed. I wanted to hear your voice. I cried. I am writing this letter as a form of therapy because I miss my family so much. I feel like I am back on track with my life though. My unit is great and makes my old unit look like shit. Our return date is 5 AUG 11.

I love you more than ever. You are the most beautiful woman in the world, and I am so happy you are mine.

I love you and miss both of you.

Love,
   James

Nancy,
            Baby, it was so nice talking to you today. I am doing a lot better than last time I wrote to you. Now I have a few friends and know where the internet cafe is. The picture of James flushing the toilet made me smile. He looks so tall and handsome. I want you to keep having people over and see your family. Things are going well for us now after a tough start. I will keep doing the right thing for our family. I feel like the man of the house has to take care of business. All I need is my woman and my boy next to me when I get back.

I love you more than ever and am proud to show off your picture.

Love,
   James

Because he was in a war zone, and being an intelligence analyst, Jim saw a lot of "fucked up shit", as he would say. With the sweet letters, sometimes the stories of blown-up bodies or sweet children selling pirated movies were included. Jim wouldn't go into much detail, but he would often tell me about waking up from nightmares of bloody bodies.

I don't know what went through Jim's mind most of the time, but what I do know is that he always had to stay busy. He often quoted an old proverb, "idle hands are the devil's playground." He'd tell me stories about his upbringing and how different he wanted to be as a father to his son. His childhood was a big mystery to me. I always craved more, and he would quickly guard it when I asked questions. So instead, I heard about fishing trips and his many high school girlfriends.

We were both too young. Quick to fall in love, quick to get married, quick to have kids. We forgot that we needed time to get to know ourselves and then each other. We separated in 2012, after one of his tours to Afghanistan. Deployment was hard, but what came after deployment was harder. I never imagined it.

One of the roughest times before our divorce, I remember I swaddled our sweet baby while singing him a melody. In the backyard, Jim was cleaning his red truck playing rap music.

He walked into the house and as he passed me, he grazed my arm and told me, "I love you".

I felt so lucky. My handsome husband was sweet. I heard him open and close the window of our room and asked what he was up to. "Don't worry about it," he said, "I was just fixing the latch. I am going to go run the truck through the carwash. I will be right back," and walked out the door. The sun was setting, and I was confused about why he needed to do that errand right at that moment.

I went back to rocking little James to sleep. I placed him gently in his crib and tiptoed out of the room to call his dad. I went to bed trusting Jim would come home soon. After a few hours, and more unanswered phone calls, I began to worry. In the back of my head I knew Jim was okay. This wasn't the first time he disappeared for the night. I knew he was likely with another woman.

One night when I was five months pregnant, Jim did not come home. There were several nights he did not come home but this time I decided to go look for him. I went to the barracks where a lot of his single friends lived and asked if anyone had seen him. The last anyone had heard he was out with one of the guys from his unit somewhere downtown. Colorado Springs is very small, so I drove through the main street and found his truck. He was not there. I went home. I couldn't sleep. I called his phone multiple times until it went straight to voicemail. I checked our bank account and saw the last transaction was for a hotel. My heart sank into a pit.

I did not go to the hotel. I drank chamomile tea from my yellow mug and went to sleep. I figured whatever he was doing was more important to him than me and my belly.

The next morning, I got a phone call from an unknown number. It was him, he needed me to pick him up.

With my hair up in a messy ponytail, puffy eyes, and

expecting the worst, I drove forty minutes to Denver to pick him up at the hotel.

"I am not raising a son on my own," I said as soon as he got in the car. "So, whatever you were doing, I hope it was the last time."

He kept his head down on the ride home and did not say one word. Once we were back home he slept for two days straight. I would check on him but did not disturb him, I just wanted him alive.

Once he woke up, as he drank a cup of dark Colombian coffee I made for him, he began to tell me about his escapade. He told me he had spent well over three thousand dollars that weekend on cocaine, alcohol, and the girls he and his friend

picked up and took to the hotel. He didn't cry, he only said he was very sorry and that it would never happen again. I believed him.

"You are my paloma negra," I said to him. He was just like the popular mariachi song. One of my favorites, before I met him. The love I longed for and looked for, as the sun rose, the love that always made me cry. That was him. He knew too, that it was my favorite song to sing.

Paloma Negra (Black Dove) by Tomas Mendez, performed by Lola Beltran, and on many occasions by me, in my living room, kitchen and car.

I am tired of crying and the dawn won't come,
I no longer know if I should curse you or pray for you,
I am afraid of searching for you and finding you,
Where your friends assure me you go to,
There are moments I would rather give up.
And tear off the nails from my grief,
But my eyes are dying without looking into your eyes,
And my affection I await for your return along with the dawn,
On your own accord you took to partying.
Black dove, black dove, where, where have you gone to now?
Stop playing with my honor.,
If your caresses have to be mine and no one else's,
And even though I am crazy in love with you, don't ever come back,
Black dove you are the grating of a penalty,
I want to be free, live my life with someone who loves me,
God give me strength, I am dying,
God give me strength; I am dying just to go and search for him.

Jim started attending counseling for his drug and alcohol problems, and by the time I gave birth, he was sober. I pretended we were a happy family, especially on social media. I pretended longer than I should have.

Another time, we were set to go on date night, and a fellow military wife was excited to babysit our sweet cheeked baby so we could go out to dinner. On the way to her house, Jim's phone persisted with numerous texts and calls. "Do you want me to answer your phone? It could be an emergency?" I said to him.

As he drove, he cleared his throat with a stern no that slammed right into my heart. He put the phone in his pocket and went silent. I knew something was strange. He was hiding something from me.

"Jim, are you cheating on me again?" I asked, with tears overflowing from my eyes now, the baby asleep in the back seat.

He immediately turned the car around within two blocks of my friend's house. I texted her, lying that the baby had a fever and we were canceling the evening. I knew she didn't believe me when she texted back asking me if I needed her to do anything or come over. I thanked her and lied that we would be okay.

When we arrived back at the apartment, Jim grabbed the baby and put him in his crib. Now disconsolate, I was yelling.

When was this going to stop? Was I not enough for him? Then, his fist bounced off my face once, sending me to the floor in disbelief. Another fist to my face, a kick in my stomach, I couldn't hear what he was saying. The room seemed to close in on me. When I stood up, my hands flying everywhere, I felt a sting on my nose. His fist sliced my skin.

I sat in the cold emergency room waiting area. Jim holding the baby in one arm, my hand with the other. With threats to take James away from me, I allowed him to take control over me. "She was opening her hatch door and because she is blind in one eye, she didn't see it coming. It just sliced her lip open." He told the reluctant admissions lady.

I wondered how I let myself get to this point, why pretending to have the perfect marriage was more important to me than my strength.

The doctor examined my cut, the slice went from my upper lip to my nose. Nothing a few stitches couldn't put back together. Me, on the other hand, that was a different story.

TO READ MORE GO TO WWW.NANCYVIERA.COM

Nancy Viera

Silhouette

Nancy Viera is the author of The Grief and The Happiness.
Her roots are from San Francisco de Borja, Chihuahua,
Mexico. She currently resides in Denver, Colorado where she
has spent most of her life. She hikes, dances and sings with
her son James and dog Troy. Nancy's books are also
translated into Spanish as it is her first language. Stay in
touch with Nancy via Instagram at Omgnancita or at
www.nancyviera.com

CPSIA information can be obtained
at www.ICGtesting.com
Printed in the USA
BVHW071950231121
622345BV00007B/395

9 780578 985718